Stuck? Unhappy?

Become the CEO of Your

Stuck? Unhappy?

Become the CEO
of Your Own Life!

Combining private and business life
in a meaningful and fruitful way.

By

Dr. Beat Buhlmann

Zug, Switzerland

2017

Bibliographical information held by the German National Library

The German National Library has listed this book in the Deutsche Nationalbibliografie (German national bibliography); detailed bibliographic information is available online at http://dnb.d-nb.de.

1st edition - Göttingen: Cuvillier, 2017

Cover Image by Lena Hürbin, Switzerland

Book Cover by Adam Renvoize, UK

© CUVILLIER VERLAG, Göttingen, Germany 2017

Nonnenstieg 8, 37075 Göttingen, Germany

Telephone: +49 (0)551-54724-0

Telefax: +49 (0)551-54724-21

www.cuvillier.de

ISBN 978-3-7369-9498-0

eISBN 978-3-7369-8498-1

Alfred Escher

(1819 – 1882)

If just more people had his wisdom,

foresight and foreknowledge…

How to Read This Book

Being aware of the scarce time of a lot of people, here a recommendation on how to read this book. If you are just interested in a rather simple but truly effective three-step life-planning/life-managing approach, in other words if you just want to know how to do it, you may directly go to chapter five.

However, if you have a bit more time and should you also be interested in understanding the underlying mechanics, the psychology behind it and why and how this approach was developed, then read the entire book.

In any case: Enjoy!

☺

Table of Contents

Table of Figures

1 Preface - Why This Book?

This book is the result of an unplanned 10-year project. Yes, you read right... unplanned. It just happened. It is a myth to believe that everything in life can be perfectly planned. Sometimes, things just happen. Working so intensively in the field of life management coaching was not planned when I started my career after graduation. However, in my first people manager role, I realized how important people management (I distinguish between *people management* and *business management*) actually is to create an environment of trust. I argue that only if a certain level of trust exists between you and your team members, a fruitful and successful long-term relationship can be established. Quick wins are easy to achieve for a manager, but anything beyond quick wins is much harder to accomplish. A mutually trusted *Manager ⇔ Team Member* relationship usually lasts longer than the actual work relationship between a team member and his or her manager - if the people management part is done well. That is one way to grow your network over time.

Having a high level of trust between a superior and the team is one way to distinguish between a manager and a leader. My personal, simplified differentiation is the following: managers just want to achieve quarterly targets to get the bonus, period. A truly long-term component does not exist in a manager's behavior and thinking. A leader, however, truly cares about people <u>and</u> the company's long-term goals, and therefore wisely balances the sometimes conflicting interests between short-term and long-term objectives as well as between team and business goals. As a result, a leader creates a true bi-directional relationship and a high level of trust which is an earned, deserved, and meaningful extension of someone's personal network – and one that you can count on also in the future. Based on my own people management experiences across different countries and cultures, I strongly believe that helping team members manage and align private and business life better is a veritable trust booster. In other words: supporting your team members with their development makes you truly stand out as a leader.

In this book, I will talk about the Swiss PDP Approach®, PDP standing for Personal Development Plan. I have been applying the Swiss PDP Approach® for many years working for Dell, Google and Evernote trying to help people combine and align private and business life in an effective and meaningful manner. I was happy to see that an actually very simple approach worked so well. I was asked by more and more Google managers around the globe to hold people development training sessions for their teams. For many reasons, Google is a wonderful company to work for, one of them being the fact that the company has a strong and real focus on developing their staff. However, there was a moment when I could not handle the training requests any more as I still had a full-time job - so I had to say "no, sorry". It was hard and kind of like against my inner believe to say "no, sorry" to something meaningful that I actually would love to do. The first person I had to say "no, sorry" to encouraged me to write a book in order to share and spread the Swiss PDP Approach®. There we go!

Acknowledgement

A big THANK YOU goes to all the people who have helped me develop and fine-tune the Swiss PDP Approach®. A special THANK YOU goes to Frank Kohl-Boas (Lead HR Business Partner, Google EMEA) and Matt Brittin (Vice-President, Google EMEA). They both truly live the values they talk about, one of their values being their genuine interest in people development. Matt's and Frank's support served as door-opener as well as an international catalyst for my people development framework within Google, finally leading to the creation of this book. Thank you both.

2   Introduction

You may argue that 'stuck' and 'unhappy' are not nice words to be the very beginning of a book title. I take that. However, it was done on purpose. The intention of this book is not to make you look at life through rose-colored glasses, but to help people make real progress. Sometimes, the truth can be brutal, but there is nothing more valuable and precious than the truth in order to make progress. In other words, the truth may often hurt[1], but it is exactly this pain that unhappy and stuck people need to wake up, to face the reality and then to finally start their improvement process. So to speak, pain is a bit like medicine. I still remember my mother when I was a preschool boy. When I was not feeling well, she gave me cod-liver oil. Those who know what cod-liver oil is know what I mean. The younger audience may potentially not know it any more thanks to the pharmaceutical industry's progress. Cod-liver oil tastes awful (first), but it helps (later)... so you choose ☺. For the more economically minded people: To make progress, the initially required pain can be seen as an investment. So let's invest and then look forward to a great return-on-investment (ROI). Therefore, I am a huge advocate and proponent of the hurt-and-rescue principle[2].

2.1   Hurt and Rescue

John Stuart Mill (1859, p. 7 ff) argued in his book "On Liberty" about a certain usefulness of the harm principle. However, as my book is supposed to be a practical handbook and not a research paper, I refrain from discussing all kinds of philosophical aspects as to the words hurt and harm. I would like to keep it

---

[1] *In this context, hurting does not mean physical harm*

[2] *http://changingminds.org/principles/hurt_rescue.htm*

simple: Facing the truth that a person is currently not happy with his or her life, often self-inflicted, <u>hurts</u>, but it gratefully often leads to a new appetite for change - that is the <u>rescue</u> part. This is the understanding of the hurt-and-rescue principle being applied in this book – nothing else.

2.2   What the Book Is and What It Is Not

This book and the Swiss PDP Approach® do <u>not</u> make a claim to be the best or the only right way to successfully manage your life or to do your life planning - but it is in the very least one possible way to do it. I argue that it is at least better than doing nothing ☺. Furthermore, it has been developed, applied, tested, further developed and fine-tuned over a period of more than ten years, in more than twelve countries around the globe and with numerous people having various cultural backgrounds. Therefore, I can say with a clear conscience it is worth a try.

The intent of this book is twofold:

a) to be an eye-opener regarding the very often heavily underestimated importance of having at least any kind of a simple life planning

   and

b) to offer people a semi-structured value finding & life planning approach that does contain some theory, but not too much. It is an applied science kind of thing that gives just the minimum instructions needed to succeed, but still leaves enough freedom to personalize the life planning according to the users' needs.

Doing so puts you in the driver's seat, and you will finally become the CEO of your own life. Far too many people are strongly influenced by others or by some societal trends, too often unwanted and unnoticed. They just go with the flow and do what is à la mode. However, it is never too late to take the driver's seat. Welcome, Ms. or Mr. CEO of your own life!

2.3   What If You Do Not Do Anything at All?

Well, you may be one of the few super-lucky people on planet earth where everything is perfectly fine, you have no tough challenges in life at all, no problems, no stress, no crises etc. Great. If you are one of these people, you can stop reading now. If not, I kindly invite you to continue.

So, enough talking... let's start now. And before I forget it... ENJOY this journey, this adventure of becoming the CEO of your own life. Do not give up, it is not even 80 pages!

3 Career Development: How It Unfortunately Often Works

Ever wondered why so many people start a career development discussion, often at work with the manager, but actually nothing really happens when you look at it afterwards? Even if something gets written down. Is it not frustrating and a huge waste of time? Numerous of my former direct reports[3] told me in the very beginning of the working relationship that they do not believe in this 'career development stuff' any more... that it is just 'hot air', just bla-bla from a company or manager trying to keep the employee temporarily happy – quite often, of course by chance, shortly before the annual employee satisfaction survey is sent out... what a coincidence!

Yes, numerous mid-size and large global companies have officially institutionalized career development frameworks in place – in theory... but how it is done, if at all, is a different story. Either way, I noticed after years of observations that in most cases, there are two main reasons why career development or people development far too often does not bring any fruitful results:

1. The **employees** themselves do not put enough emphasis on career development discussions, and let it go or postpone it on a regular basis – even over years. Maybe they are a bit lazy, maybe they are in their comfort zone, or they may have unsuccessfully tried it several times, became frustrated and finally gave up.

---

[3] *A term widely used by American companies. It stands for all team members (directly) reporting to their manager. In other words: a manager leads a team of direct reports.*

2. Numerous **managers** either do not like this topic because they may have short-term goals with the company themselves (so no interest in developing a person, just looking forward to the next big quarterly bonus and then exit), or they simply do not know how to do it due to lack of knowhow and training.

Well, we cannot change what has happened in the past, but we can for sure influence the future. Therefore, let's stop moaning and move on. First, we want to understand why most of today's used career development approaches fail, and then we will fix it. Stay tuned!

3.1 Issue One: Why the Term 'Career Development' Does Actually Not Make Sense

It already begins with the name. I argue that the term 'career development' is misleading and already one source of the evil. In my opinion, one cannot just look at developing his or her career (I use the terms career and work-life interchangeably) without taking the entire life situation of a person into account. Why? Well, you are <u>one</u> human being, you do not live in two completely separated silos *private-life* and *work-life*. In other words: What happens in *private-life* may have in impact on your *work-life* and vice versa. Certain 'things' or your values of one world may have an influence on the other world. Have you thought about it? See issue two.

3.2 Issue Two: The Wall… But There Is No Wall Between Work and Life

The often used term 'work-life balance' connotes and implies that there is kind of a wall between work and (private) life – which is simply not the case. Living in today's world of internet and smartphones with its cognitive information overload from various sources (private and business) causing a tremendous amount of interruptions, can we still sharply split between working time and private time? I do not think so. Things you do or things that happen in your private life may influence your work-life to a certain degree, and vice versa, e.g. your hobby, having a baby, a tough sickness, an accident, a nasty divorce fight etc. We are human beings and cannot simply switch things on and off like a software or a robot, we cannot jump from one world to the other one. E.g. people being in a nasty divorce fight may not be able to turn that part completely off during working hours. Further, it also affects overall happiness, physical condition, willingness to go the extra-mile etc. Of course, the job may also affect your private or family life, e.g. long working hours, doing emails in the evening, working half of the weekend etc. So in our thinking, let's tear down this virtual wall between *work-life* and *private-life* and let's just talk about *life*.

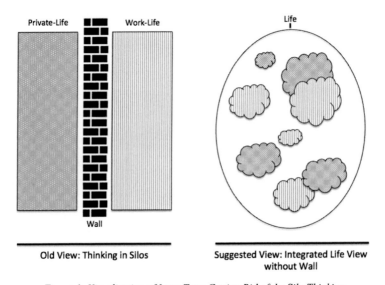

Figure 1: Visualization of Issue Two: Getting Rid of the Silo Thinking

3.3 Issue Three: Starting With Step Two Instead of Step One

"First walk, then run" – I will never forget what my first Google manager, Dr. Andreas Schönenberger, told me many times. He was so right. What does it have to do with people development? Based on my experience, one of the main reasons why development approaches are far too often not successful is the simple fact that most of these approaches start with the 2nd step instead of the 1st one. Hmm... 2nd step? Yes. Comparing at least 15 different development approaches being used at companies (Dell, HP, Google, IBM, Unilever etc.) or being taught at schools, most of them directly start with something like: "What do you want to do in five years from now?" or "Where do you see yourself in five or ten years from now?". Let's be honest: Who liked these questions at the beginning of a career or development meeting with the manager? Who can answer this question at this stage? Do not get me wrong, it is not a bad or a wrong question, but... it is simply not the right moment to ask this kind of question. So please do not start your career discussion like that.

One killer argument of the Swiss PDP Approach® is its focus on the person *first* and the development *second*. Even though a development discussion is actually all about the person, it looks like in many cases, that gets kind of overlooked quite often. How should you be able to even start thinking about career or general development needs and next steps if beforehand you have not spent some time getting to know yourself better and finding out about yourself? Who are you actually? What are your values, and what should your 'brand' stand for? It is like building a house. You cannot start with the roof – where do you want to put it if there are no walls?

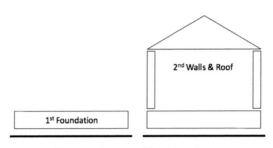

Figure 2: Process of Building a House

The first step of a building construction is a solid foundation, then the walls, then finally the roof. The same is true for your PDP: you need a solid foundation (=> knowing who you are), then it makes sense to continue, but not before.

Once you know who you actually are, things you want or do not want to be part of your 'brand', and how you want to be perceived (that's all the 1st step), then you can do the 2nd step and start the development process – shown in Figure 3. Again: 'First walk, then run'. Babies do it the same way, and it seems to make a lot of sense.

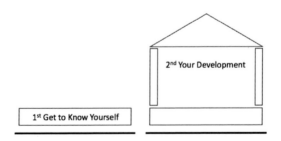

Figure 3: Swiss PDP Approach® Analogy to Building a House

3.4 How to Address the Above-Mentioned Issues regarding Development Approach?

It is time to get our hands dirty and do some work – let's fix the above-mentioned issues. I like simple things, so let's keep it simple here, too.

- First, we do not talk about *career development* anymore. **Issue one**: done.
- Then, as of now, we will make sure that we keep a holistic view of the situation and do not think in private silo and work silo. **Issue two**: done.
- Last, we simply start with step one instead of step two. We will therefore start with the person and not with a list of potential next steps or potential trainings an employee could do. **Issue three**: done.

That was not so hard, it seems. However, we all know there is a difference between theory and practice, between intention and doing. We have the right intention, great, now let's focus on execution and implementation.

Basic Rules of PDP Success:

1) You do not need a company, a manager or your mom to start managing your life – it starts with YOU! If want to become the CEO of your own life, act accordingly. **ACT!**

2) You are in the driver's seat, so you are responsible for making sure about next steps and getting them done. Of course, you may ask for external help, but the **LEAD** stays with **YOU**.

3) **NEVER BLAME OTHERS** like your manager, your parents, your friends, your internet provider, the tax officer, your government, your company, your girlfriend/boyfriend, the milkman etc. Of course, the

company's strategy, the school system, superordinate goals, laws, your DNA etc. have an influence on you and your success, but just blaming others without taking actions does not make you move on. Blaming others or blaming a circumstance may give you a temporary relieve, but it does not fix the problem, unfortunately. It never does. Never!

Summary

Before we move on, let's summarize and then of course apply what he have learned so far:

- We will start with the 1st step, not the 2nd: Let's get a solid foundation first => Who are you?
- We will tear down the virtual wall between private-life and work-life. Let's start with a holistic view of life: just LIFE.
- We will put you in the driver's seat – there is no other way to become CEO of your life.
- We will not blame others. We know it does not help… so let's not do it (anymore).

4   Grandfather's Wisdom

I just have to add this tiny, little chapter. It is such a striking insight of life, also regarding management theory, even if it apparently seems to be a very simple one. As often said: small & simple things can make a huge difference.

My grandfather told and taught me many things, but this one here stroke me most – and proved to be so right:

> *The main difference between adults and kids is the height, and not the behavior.*

Wow… read it again, and then reflect a moment… what a powerful insight… and so true! When I heard it the first time as a kid, I did not really understand it. The older I got and the more I saw how adults behave, independent of their age or seniority level within a company, the more I had to admit: it is so bloody true. Over the years, I have observed the same basic behavioral patterns amongst kids and adults – sometimes so silly behavioral patterns of not admitting a mistake, heavily overestimating one's own strengths, ignoring blind spots and weaknesses, blaming others, trying to manipulate others or trick the system... the list is long.

4.1   Back to Business: What Is the 'So What' of Grandfather's Statement?

The more management experience I have gained, and the more I have reflected after having survived management challenges, problem situations or even crises, the clearer it became: the main drivers and key behaviors of adults and kids are not so different, if different at all. Example: In the sandbox, kids fight about toys and sand shovels etc. In companies, adults fight for who has the parking slot closest to the entry door, the nicest laptop, the more expensive company car, the coolest smart phone etc. With regards to jealousy, it is the same underlying mechanism that you need to understand whether you deal with kids and adults. In other words and admittedly a bit ironic: it is basically the same 'kindergarten', with one exception: Kids show their behavior very transparently e.g. by taking the toy away, slapping each other, or by telling you to the face "I don't like you! You are bad!". Harsh but honest. Adults, on the other side, may play games with hidden agendas, sometimes even dirty ones, and talk behind other people's back. So be prepared!

The lessons learned here are very simple:

1) **BASICS**: When dealing with people, do not overcomplicate your management analysis. Before you go into details and launch a series of highly complex measures, think whether you have a) truly understood the big picture of the situation and b) taken into account the basics of human behavior (here, it may be a good idea to quickly google 'Maslow pyramid wiki' and read it. For those who already know it, you may read his theory of basic human needs again, it may be a good refresher. Even though Maslow's theory is quite old, not always 100% applicable, and more and more researcher challenge his theory, it still gives you at least a simple foundation of the theory of needs).

   => **Apply Grandfather's wisdom:** Of course, dealing with adults, you may use a different vocabulary than dealing with kids, but the rest…

2) **BE HONEST WITH YOURSELF**: Back to your personal development, make sure you are honest with yourself and reflect: how often have you

behaved, and this may sound hard and harsh, at kindergarten level? Playing jealousy games, talking behind someone's back etc.? As the 1st step is to get to know yourself better, in other words to have a solid foundation, you have to become self-aware of your own behaviors. Then, decide which ones you want to keep, and which ones you want to get rid of.

=> **Action:** Please take some notes here, you will use them later. Write down whatever comes to your mind with regards to your behavior – and yes, you need to write down things you are not proud of, too… Take 5 to 10 minutes, then move on.

5 Let's Fix It: Introducing the Swiss PDP Approach®

First things first: believe it or not, the name Swiss PDP Approach® was not my idea. After having shown my PDP approach to a Googler based in another country, he said: "Aha, that is the Swiss PDP Approach". He then told others about it, so a bit later I was asked to give a *Swiss PDP Approach* training to another Google sales teams. The name was born. You may argue whether or not it is the ideal name. Probably not. At least, people seem to remember it. If you have a better name for it, please let me know (beat.buhlmann@gmail.com). But now let's hit the *start* button!

Figure 4: PDP Start Button

Let's keep the book title in mind. You want to become the CEO of your own life, to be in the driver's seat. Let's stick to the CEO analogy for a bit. A company's CEO has to know the industry eco-system and the competitive landscape, no doubt about it. That is the outside view. Very useful, very important. Further, a CEO also needs to have the inside view. What are strengths and weaknesses of the company, advantages and disadvantages compared to competitors. Moreover, to be able to steer a company into the right and desired direction, a CEO also needs to know the vision as well as the mission statement, usually coming from the board of the company. So once a CEO knows what the company wants to achieve, what values the company stands for and what milestones should be reached, then the CEO will set priorities and define next steps… and for you who want to become the CEO of your own life, we are going to do the same thing in the same order: finding out what you stand for and what your vision & mission are, then setting priorities, and finally move on to 'execution mode'. Or as we have already talked about earlier: Starting with step one (not two), so first walk then run. The following diagram visualizes the three steps:

| 3rd Step: Craft Your Next Steps |
| 2nd Step: Set Your Priorities |
| 1st Step: Get to Know Yourself |

Figure 5: The Three Main Steps of the Swiss PDP Approach®

Do not worry, you do not need to already fully understand why there are these three steps. The diagram just serves as an orientation for you. Let's now start with step one.

5.1 Step One: Who Are You? ⇒ Creating Your Life-Map

Welcome to the first step of your Swiss PDP adventure. Objective of step one is that you get to know yourself. That may sound obvious and easy, but it is usually not. However, it is crucial… and a super-interesting task, too.

To reach our objective, you will first create your **life-map**. A life-map is actually a double mind-map: a *private mind-map* and a *professional mind-map* on one page (for those who have never heard about mind-maps, please google "mind maps wiki" and read the Wikipedia article prior to proceeding). Why not having two papers, each mind-map on a separate paper? Please remember issue two: nowadays, there is no strict wall between private-life and work-life.

Therefore, it is crucial to have the big picture on one page in order to connect the dots and finally make meaningful decisions. A double mind-map on one large sheet of paper suits this purpose well.

While we just clarified why we start with a double mind-map on one paper, one question remains: why mind-maps at all? The advantages of starting with a mind-map approach are:

- Loosely structured, brainstorming kind of approach, but still something in writing to stay and work with later
- Highly visual (the way our brain works better)
- No need to already talk about timing and priorities (not yet, at least... ☺)
- Later on, you can circle things, add arrows to make connections between various elements, so you can actually work with your thoughts

Before we can start, please read and carefully follow the five instructions:

1. Take an **A3 sheet of paper** (A3 format is double A4. For people from non-metric countries: double a letter size). Why so large? You will need a lot of space, a normal sheet of paper is not enough. Believe me.
2. Take **two pens** of different colors
3. **Turn off** your smart phone... I know it is hard... please turn it off... also not on vibration. Fully off. Even better: Place your phone in another room.
4. **Turn off** your computer or laptop. That means no Facebook, Outlook, Netflix, Skype, SnapChat, Instagram, YouTube etc.
5. Go to a place with **zero distractions**: no friends, kids, girlfriend, boyfriend or any other kind of partner, TV, radio, postman, milkman etc. and then have a seat. Take a deep breath.

Ready? Great. Let's continue.

6. Please write your name in the middle of the paper, and circle it.

7. Then add two circles, one to the left and one to the right, and name them 'private' and 'professional'. Use one color for 'private' and another one for 'professional'. Your paper should look more or less like Figure 6.

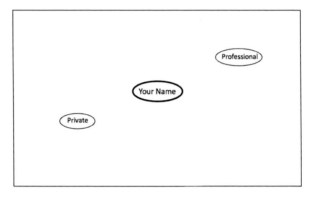

Figure 6: A3 Sheet of Paper with Your Double Mind-Map – the Start

8. Start your mind-map style brainstorming for your private part (one color) and for your business part (another color). Be courageous, do not think too long, just give it a go. For both areas, think about things that you liked a lot in the past, things or people that impressed you much, or things that you are actually inspired/motivated to do but have never done yet. Do not think about the 'why", just write down your wishes, dreams, issues, disappointments, good experiences, but also the bad ones. Be yourself, be honest, and do not be shy. This may take about 30min, sometimes even more. Take your time. It is worth it… FYI: you are working on your PDP foundation.

9. Should you be a bit confused, that is ok… that is actually always the case. So, no worries. Continue reading. Do not give up, keep going! I will help

you a bit. Please have a look at Appendix 1 at the end of this book. Appendix 1 contains three exercises from a famous German psychologist called Tanja Konnerth that will help you find out who you are. So instruction 9 is enriching your current life-map with the outcomes of these three exercises. Advice: Please *do* invest the time for the three exercises in Appendix 1, do not skip them. Getting to know yourself is instrumental, it is the foundation of your PDP.

Before we move on, I will show you an example how a life-map may look like. Please have a look at the following page. This is a real-life example of a London-based Googler who chose the Swiss PDP Approach® for his development plan. The only thing I removed, of course, was the name of the person[4].

=> CAUTION - WARNING

- Very important: this is just an **example**.
- Please **do not** be influenced by the **content** of this life-map. Every person is different, so every life-map looks different, and that is ok.
- Do not copy-paste, it would ruin the entire exercise. Develop your own life-map.

---

[4] *The Googler was of course asked for his permission to use his example for training purposes.*

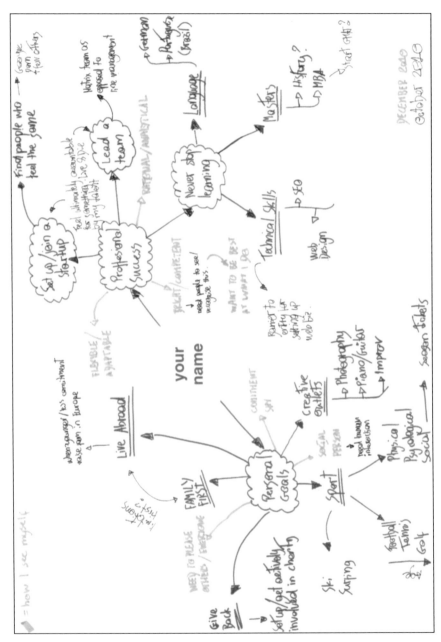

Figure 7: Example of a Real Life-Map

31

As you can see, this person used red for private and blue for professional[5]. Please ignore for the time being the colors green and black, we will talk about them later on.

Further Instructions:

10. After having studied the example life-map, invest another 10-20min and further develop your own life-map. While you should not blindly copy-past from the example, I may still have triggered some ideas. You decide.

11. Then take a short break. It is a good moment to drink something or to go for a walk, **BUT** do not turn on your smart phone or computer – be a good student ☺. Why? Focus is key... We know it... Whatever has happened during the last hour or so, the likelihood that it is more important than what you are doing here (finding out who you are... building your PDP foundation) is probably below 0.00001%. If you still do not believe me regarding 'focus is key', then please read the book 'Deep Work' from Cal Newport (2016) – it will convince you... guaranteed!

12. Now, look at your life-map again and analyze it. Anything that surprises you, or anything that contradicts? What is missing?

5.1.1 *Working With Your Life-Map: From Version 1.0 to Version 3.0*

Congratulations on your life-map version 1.0. Yes, it is version 1.0 and more versions will follow later on. Do not forget, this exercise is about getting to

---

[5] *Are you good at orthography? Did you spot the spelling mistake in his life-map?*
Proffesional is written with a double-f instead of a double-s. I decided not to use photoshop to correct it, I wanted to keep the original version as it was.

know yourself, so it is a discovery journey, not just a quick-and-dirty one-step exercise.

In order to get the most out of this exercise, and to get to life-map version 2.0, you need some help - you need other people. You will need to choose at least two to three people of trust. People that know you from different points of view. Make sure you choose people who are honest, direct and who tell you the truth. Do not choose people who simply say *yes* to everything or people who just want to please you. You need **challengers**... tough guys. Not physically tough guys, but mentally tough guys... experienced people saying the truth. The following diagram visualizes the process to get from version 1.0 to version 2.0:

Figure 8: Life-Map: How to Get from Version 1.0 to Version 2.0

One of these challengers could be your manager, but it does not have to. This would be ideal, but it only works if there is certain level of trust. Up to you. So far, all my direct reports in the past happily shared their life-maps with me[6]. For a people manager truly interested in developing its team members, that is the ideal case. However, it would also work without having your direct manager as one of your challengers. Important is that you discuss your life-map with two to

---

[6] *Showing a Life-Map to a manager may not work in all countries, either for cultural or even for legal reasons. Make sure you doublecheck the situation in your country and company before offering your team members to share their Life-Map with you.*

three people. In other words: set up individual meetings with each of the three challengers and talk them through your thoughts – step by step – but also give them chances to ask questions and, most importantly, to challenge you. What does *challenge you* mean? They should ask you why you want to do something, or why not, or why you have actually written a specific thing on the life-map, but also challenge you if an element might be missing. What made you write it down? Why are you convinced that a certain step/idea/hobby/objective makes sense? Have you thought about alternatives, e.g. alternative ideas or alternative ways of achieving something?

Two Real Challenger Examples – aka Tasks of a Life-Map Challenger
Example 1: Please have a look at the real example of a life-map above. I was one of his three challengers. I will tell you what I asked him. Please go to the red personal goals part. There, you can see that he wrote "Family First".

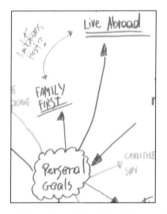

Figure 9: Detecting a Visualized Contradiction

I asked him: "What do you mean by that? Tell me more." He answered: "You know, my mother died during my birth. I was raised by my grandmother. She is very important to me. She is now very old and sick. I will, for sure, stay in London as long as she lives. I want to see her regularly and help her as much as I can." Interesting… why? Well, a bit later, he told me that he wants to live abroad as fast as possible. He was very excited about living abroad for a while. USA or Canada, he was dreaming of. That was a crucial moment, and a moment that required an instant 'wait a moment' from the challenger… "Wait a moment… You cannot stay in London *and* move abroad at the same time, that is a contradiction!" You should have seen his face. It may seem obvious once you map it out (that is actually the power of mapping things out…), but in the daily life of busy people living in a world of multi-distractions and heavy cognitive overloads, it happens quite often that people do not see the simplest contradictions. So on one day, he was dreaming of going abroad asap, and then the next day, it was crystal-clear to him to stay in London as his grandmother needs him. In other words, he was silo-dreaming or silo-thinking. He needed my side-kick to make him aware of this contradiction – kind of a wake-up call. In the next chapter about step two, I will tell you how we resolved that contradiction issue.

Example 2: Please have a look at the same example life-map again, but this time look to the right, at the blue professional part "never stop learning". There, you can see that he wrote "Masters" and then "MBA".

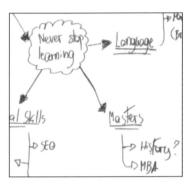

Figure 10: Detecting a Go-With-the-Flow Problem

I challenged him why he wants to do an MBA. He came up with a lot, sorry for the term, blabla. I asked him again: "Tell me why you wrote MBA underneath Masters. Why do you want to get an MBA degree? What is the problem you try to solve by getting an MBA degree? What was your decision-making-process which led you to write the three letters MBA here?" I had to be tough with him... He starred at me for quite a moment, then he admitted: "Beat, I do not really know why I wrote MBA." I thanked him for his honest answer. I then challenged him a bit more: "Is there a chance that you wrote MBA because nowadays, virtually everyone talks about MBA? Did you write MBA just because it is *à la mode* at the moment? Did you just go with the flow without really reflecting what the problem is that you try to solve getting an MBA?" He was nodding and admitted "Yes..." He felt bad. It almost broke my heart, but I had to do it... Do you remember the Hurt and Rescue Principle I mentioned in the beginning of the book? This story here is a great example of Hurt and Rescue. I pushed him really hard. He even felt bad... but it was an eye-opener... it was hurting to admit that he just went with the flow and wrote MBA just because it is currently à la mode. That is also the task of a challenger: open his or her eyes... show them the truth, even if it hurts – or actually because it hurts, because only if it hurts a bit, you get people out of their comfort zone… and that is **the best place to be to make progress**.

Do you want to know how we resolved this issue? ☺ Sure… I asked him: "Amongst all the things you like, what do you like doing most?" It took us a moment to get to the answer, but he finally said: "I love working with numbers. I am a numbers guy." After another 5 minutes of discussion, we figured out that a Master of Finance degree instead of a Master of Business Administration degree is what he should actually do. Yes, a Master of Finance may not sound as cool and glamourous as an MBA, but hey… do you want to please others, or do you want to be the CEO of your own life? It is your choice… and he made his choice. I think the right one[7].

The two examples show it clearly: You absolutely need to do the sessions with your challengers in order to detect potential blind spots, to be challenged as well as to get the external view (e.g. how you, your skill set or your behavior is perceived externally). Compare their views with how you see yourself or how you see things. Is there a delta? If yes, why? What is the root cause for this different consideration, the different view? Work on that, it is crucial. The more you do that, the more stable your foundation becomes. You want a solid and stable foundation, right? So work hard and get challenged as much as possible. By the way: If it does not hurt a bit from time to time, you were not challenged enough => restart!

Once you have discussed your life-map 1.0 with all your challengers individually, you can make amendments and do some fine-tuning, finally

---

[7] *Underline: When* *he should do his Master of Finance degree is not part the first step (the Life-Map), but the 2nd step (Life-Cycle Model).*

leading to life-map version 2.0. That is a big step as by now, you have added the crucial external views, and you should have been challenged quite a bit ☺.

How to Get to Version 3.0

In one of the corners of your life-map, write the things that you absolutely do not want to do or do not want to have experienced in your life. I call it the *no-go list*. This will give you a hint regarding your core values. Here some examples I have seen over time:

- No heart attack because of being constantly overworked
- BMI index never above 25
- Not getting divorced because of my job
- Spending little to no time with my kids
- I will not work for extreme capitalists (banks, petroleum companies)
- etc.

Whatever is important to you, write it down. I am serious: write it down. Once it is written, it is more binding. It helps you in the future whenever you have to make a tough decision. It is like a self-written reminder for yourself which should prevent you from doing something against your own beliefs and values, maybe because of a short-term and lucrative opportunity or because someone else influences you.

I am sure you are a good student, right? So you did the three exercises in Appendix 1 mentioned earlier in Chapter 5.1. Why? The outcome of these three exercises should have revealed quite a bit about your core values and beliefs. They help you now create your no-go list.

The following diagram visualizes the entire process getting from version 1.0 to version 3.0:

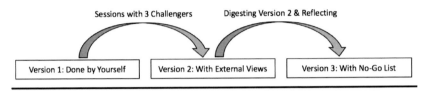

Figure 11: Life-Map Process Overview: Getting from Version 1.0 to Version 3.0

Getting to life-map version 3.0 takes some time. I suggest that you put it away for a couple of days and do not think about it. Take a break. Get some 'intellectual fresh air'. You are not in a rush. Rome was not built in a day, too. Good things take time. After a couple of days, look again at your life-map. Review what is written there and check the no-go list that you put in one of the corners. Still everything ok? Anything to add, or maybe even to strike through? Also this may happen. FYI this is YOUR life-map. You can write, add and strike through as you like. It is a working paper, an ongoing project that will change as you grow – and get older ☺. Also, it will never be perfect, and it does not have to be. It cannot be perfect. Life cannot be planned in its entirety, but you may still be in the driver's seat of your life, steering your boat the way you want despite strong currents, wind, rain or other influences.

5.1.2 What You Get from Your Life-Map

As you now have version 3.0, it is time to think about what you get out of your life-map. Of course, the creation of the life-map and the discussions with your two to three challengers will already have given you some new insights and external input. It should also have helped identify potential blind spots. However, there is more about it. Earlier, I promised to get back to the green and black color of the real life-map example of a Googler from my team in London – do you remember? He used different colors (green and black) to visualize how his life-map has developed/evolved over time. In other words, you may plan to review your life-map every year, e.g. around new year, and add things in a different color. That way, you are able to track the evolution of your life-map. Look at the corner to the bottom right of the example life-map: He wrote *December 2010* in green and **October 2010** in black, and then added new content using these colors. It is up to you if you would like to do this or not. Again, it is your life-map, and you are the CEO of your own life. Make a decision.

5.2   Step Two: Set Priorities ⇒ Creating Your Life-Cycle Model

Congratulations again. Your life-map version 3.0 is done. You now have a solid foundation of yourself, your aspirations, wishes, goals, no-gos etc., all of that well challenged by three people of your choice. We now move on to step two: the **life-cycle model**. Objective of step two is to transform the loosely developed, non-prioritized and brainstorming style life-map into something that helps you prioritize. We all know: one cannot do 20 things at the same time. Focus is key, and focus will result in GTD[8] (Getting Things Done). In other words, we will convert your life-map into a life-cycle model by adding a new dimension: the time. Why? Adding a time dimension will force you to prioritize what you are going to do in the current life-cycle, and what you may do later or maybe even never. Welcome to the tough process of setting priorities! Yay...

---

[8] *GTD: term created by David Allen https://en.wikipedia.org/wiki/Getting_Things_Done*

So let's start:

1. Also here, take an A3 sheet of paper and two pens of different color.

2. First, at the bottom, draw a horizontal line which will serve as the time axis (like the x-axis in mathematics). Use the color of your choice for that.

3. Then, on the left-hand side, draw a vertical line (like the y-axis in mathematics). Use the <u>same</u> color here as you did for the x-axis.

4. Afterwards, add two vertical divider lines which will serve as dividers between short-term, medium-term and long-term actions/ideas. Use the same color here again. Your paper should now look more or less like this:

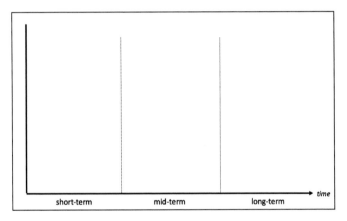

Figure 12: Preparing your A3 Sheet of Paper for Step Two, the Life-Cycle Model

5. Now the interesting part of step two begins: transforming your life-map into your life-cycle model. Just look at your life-map: take everything, step-by-step, and try to place it into the life-cycle model. As we now have a time dimension, it forces you to start thinking about priorities (time-wise): what do you want to do/achieve short-term, what mid-term and what long-term? Are there any interdependencies? In other words: If you want to do X, does X require anything to be done beforehand? E.g. if you

41

want to get your driver's license (X), you first need to pass an eye test before you can apply for your driver's license. It is a tough exercise, I know. Do not be afraid of making mistakes – it is your life-cycle model, you may make changes afterwards as you wish.

6. Are you a bit confused what step two is all about? No worries, it is part of the game. Keep going. You will soon see how useful and eye-opening your life-cycle model is. Do not give up!

Also here, before we move on, I will show you an example how a life-cycle model may look like. Please have a look at the following page. This is the real example of the same London-based Googler who chose the Swiss PDP Approach® for his development plan.

=> CAUTION - WARNING

- Very important: this is just an **example**.
- Please **do not** be influenced by the **content** of this life-cycle model. Every person is different, so every life-cycle model looks different, and that is ok.
- Do not copy-paste, it would ruin the entire exercise. Develop your own life-cycle model.

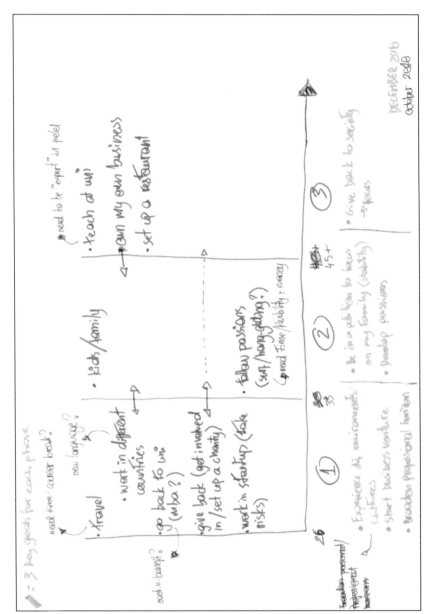

Figure 13: Example of a Real Life-Cycle Model

43

As you can see, this person used the numbers 1, 2 and 3 indicating the three life-cycles instead of short-term, medium-term and long-term. That is fine. Again, it is your life-cycle model. Feel free to play around, however, ideally without changing the main principle of having several life-cycles. FYI some people choose to have three, some four, and very few just two life-cycles – up to you, but I suggest starting with three, and later on, you may change the number of life-cycles if you wish.

Further instructions:

7. After having studied the life-cycle model example, invest another 10-20min and further develop your own life-cycle model. Use the example as inspiration only, do not copy-paste without thinking.

8. Then take a short break. It is a good moment to eat or drink something or to go for a walk, **BUT** do not turn on your cell phone or computer – be a good student ☺. Why? Again: Focus is still key… We still know it… And again: Whatever has happened during the last hour or so, the likelihood that it is more important than what you are doing here (creating your PDP) is probably below 0.00001%.

9. Then, after the break, look at your life-cycle model again and analyze it. Anything that surprises you, or anything that does not make sense? Anything even missing? If yes, write it down. Work with your life-cycle model, enrich it, modify it, enhance it. Enjoy!

5.2.1 Working With Your Life-Cycle Model: From Version 1.0 to Version 3.0

Congratulations on your life-cycle model version 1.0. Also here, you will again need the help of your challengers (ideally the same) to make sure you have enough external input to prevent blind spots, to get challenged as much as you can, and to get as much input from experienced people as possible.

Figure 14: Life-Cycle Model: How to Get from Version 1.0 to Version 2.0

The challengers will enrich your life-cycle model the same way they enriched your life-map in step one.

Three Real Challenger Examples: Tasks of a Life-Cycle Model Challenger

Example 1: Seeing the big picture. Please have a look at the example of the life-cycle model above. You may remember: I was one of his three challengers. So in another session, we jointly looked at his life-cycle model, and I did what I can do best: challenging him… or as we say in German: put the finger into the wound. That is an expression stating that it needs to hurt to get out of the comfort zone, to really highlight an issue, or to get them a wake-up call in order to bring him back to reality.

Please look at his first life-cycle, the short-term life-cycle, in Figure 15.

Figure 15: The Common Trap: Short-Term Life-Cycle Too Crowded

What do you see looking at his life-cycle one and comparing it with life-cycles two and three? Well, it looks quite crowded in his life-cycle one, right? So many things are written there... too many... that is a common trap: most people cannot wait and want everything right away. It has almost become kind of an illness nowadays, this 'I want everything right away' kind of behavior. Well, it is what it is, we have to deal with it. And also here, you can see the power of visualizing: everyone can easily recognize that there is too much on the plate in life-cycle one. No one can handle that.

Another good thing of visualizing your thoughts in your life-cycle model is the fact that people see and realize most issues themselves - because it is visualized. I did not need to tell him that it is impossible to achieve what is written in life-cycle one, he realized it himself right away. There is no way:

- to stay in London for his Grandmother and, at the same time…
- … to live abroad,
- to found a charity organization (he did not have any money, by the way),
- to get a Master Degree (at least he figured out that it should be a Master of Finance…),
- to work in a start-up,
- to do all this besides his normal daily life,

and everything more or less at the same time. You may imagine that it did not take much time for him to see, understand and agree: Houston, we have a problem – we need to tidy up.

Example 2: Fixing the *staying-in-London* versus *living-abroad* contradiction. Now please look at the upper part of his life-cycle one. There, you can see that he wrote 'work in different countries'.

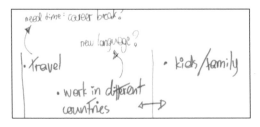

Figure 16: Upper Part of Life-Cycle One

Do you remember that he wrote 'Family First' on his life-map? The thing about his grandmother? And that he was dreaming of living & working abroad asap? I promised to tell you later how we resolved that issue – here we go. As one of his challengers, I told him again that this contradiction has to be solved. After some talking, he made a clear statement: "As long as my grandmother is here, I stay in

London – period.". Great. Clear statements help. He made a call. For those who like mathematics: he turned a variable into a constant. Equations with fewer variables are much easier to solve, right? ☺ As staying in London during the short-term life-cycle was decided, we continued the discussion about living abroad. He still wanted to do it… and look what he did himself? Look at the black circle in the following picture:

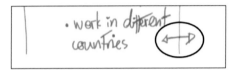

Figure 17: Moving an Item to Another Life-Cycle

He moved his wish to live and work abroad from the current life-cycle to the next one[9]. That is another super-strong asset of working with a visualized life-cycle model: you can move things around… around the timeline. You can move items to a later stage or to an earlier stage, as you wish – but there is even more! When you move something to the next life-cycle, it also means that it frees up your current life-cycle you are working on at the moment. Less things in a life-cycle automatically means more focus, and focus is key for GTD (Getting-Things-Done). He did not abandon his intention of living and working abroad, but he moved it to a later stage because of his decision to stay in London as long as his grandmother is alive[10]. By the way, once he moved the going abroad thing

---

[9] *You may have noticed that he drew a double arrow. He first hesitated a bit, that is the reason for the double arrow indicating that he first wanted to keep the option of moving it back open. Later, it removed the left arrowhead to make it clear.*

[10] *One may argue that it is quite hard to say or plan 'I will do x as long as person y is alive'. I agree. However, welcome to the real world. Things like that just happen. Face the reality. Life is not a bed of roses all the time.*

to the next life-cycle, he asked me: "Did I not just gain some time by moving something to the next life-cycle?". I said "Yeah! What is on your mind?" Another wonderful thing about visualizing just happened: In his brain, the move of his intention to live abroad to the next life-cycle freed up something in his brain and triggered a new idea: he could use the time he will spend in London to learn a new language – that way, he would have more options for living abroad, not just English speaking countries... he was so excited about this new opportunity which just appeared that he decided to learn Spanish... and he really learned Spanish, as he told me later. How great is that? All of that great thinking and deciding happened because he worked with his life-map, his life-cycle model and with challengers. By now, you should clearly see the value-add of the Swiss PDP Approach®. But there is more, read the next example.

Example 3: Fixing the *creating-a-charity-organization* issue as no money was available at all. The UK-Googler was truly a good guy, a great young man. He wanted to do something good. He told me: "Beat, I was so lucky to be born in London and to have had the chance to go to a University – I have to give something back to society, I have to do a charity thing." So nice... good guy. So what to do? He told me about all the good things his charity organization should do. I then did the math and told him: "If you want to do all that, you need at least... at least half a million £." He was speechless... he had good intensions, but no cash... now look at the following picture to see what he decided to do.

Figure 18: Fixing His Charity Ambition & Cash Problem

He moved his intention to set up a charity organization to the next life-cycle, life-cycle two (mid-term). Further, he even added a dotted line to the last life-cycle, life-cycle three (long-term). One may ask: Is he now not a good guy anymore? Not at all. He still wants to set up a charity organization, but he needs cash – so he will do it later. However, after having discussed a bit, he still wanted to do good things now. Good things that do not require cash, however. After a bit of joint brainstorming, I suggested to him the following: "Hey, why not help an elderly person in your neighborhood? You may offer this person to do the weekly grocery shopping, for instance. I am sure the elderly person would appreciate not only the help with shopping, but also the time you spend with him/her. Lastly, it does not require cash, just some time and goodwill. Bingo.

Back to your PDP. Once you have discussed your life-cycle model 1.0 with all your challengers individually, you can make amendments and do some fine-tuning, finally leading to life-cycle model version 2.0. That is a big step as by now, you have again added the crucial external views, and you should have again been challenged quite a bit ☺.

How to Get to Version 3.0
There is one more thing we need to add to your life-cycle model in order to complete it. It is something that most people do not consciously think about it: the cash burn-rate. The following diagram visualizes the entire life-cycle model process.

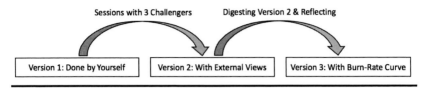

Figure 19: Life-Cycle Model Process Overview: Getting from Version 1.0 to Version 3.0

What is the cash burn-rate, and what the cash burn-rate curve? The term burn-rate comes from the finance industry. Let's look at it like your monthly fixed cost. Think about the amount of money you spend monthly to live your life. The process of *spending money* is often called *burning money*, because once your money is spent, it is gone – like burnt.

Anyway, let's move on to the actual meaning for your PDP. I use the following simplified life consideration approach to explain the cash burn-rate <u>curve</u>:

- When you are a kid, your parents pay everything.
- Then, as a student or young adult, you usually live a very cost-conscious life – in other words, you do not burn a lot of money, but still more compared to the time when you were a kid => so your cash burn-rate goes up a bit.
- Then, a lot of people get a degree and start earning money. At the same time, their standard of living increases, so at the end of the day, you usually spend more money per month compared to the time as a student. Again, your burn-rate goes up.
- Later, you may get married, may have kids, may buy a house and therefore need a mortgage, and last but not least, you may have to start saving money to pay for your kids' education/university. That is usually the cash burn-rate peak when you need and spend the most money per month. In other words, you have very high fixed cost per month.

The following diagram visualizes the raise of the burn-rate over time.

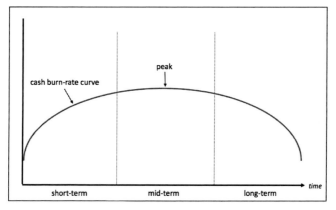

Figure 20: Introducing a New Term: Cash Burn-Rate Curve

However, if you looked carefully at the curve, you may have noticed something: after the peak, it does not stay at the peak level... it is decreasing. What may look obvious is actually something important that a lot of people, even very intelligent ones, do not always take into account. Once your kids get their degrees and the house is fully or at least partially paid (=> lower mortgage => lower mortgage interest), you will gain something crucial: more financial freedom, or more financial flexibility. In the next diagram, you will see a grey area that symbolizes the financial freedom/flexibility you will have gained over time.

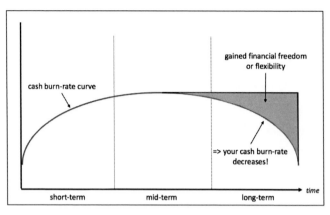

Figure 21: Attempt to Visualize the Gained Financial Freedom Over Time

In other words: your fixed cost becomes lower. Why is this so important? Well, the older generations have always lived the dogma of 'the older you get, the more you have to climb the career ladder and the more you have to earn – period'. Looking at the cash burn-rate curve, that does not really make sense, as your fixed cost will decrease significantly in most cases. There is no law, at least not to my knowledge, that forces you to earn more and more the older you get. Think about it... it is totally up to you, the CEO of your own life.

Why is the fact of a decreasing cash burn-rate important? Having financial freedom/flexibility will spark your imagination. You may make very unusual, but great and super-exciting decisions, like you may plan for and then later on also accept lower paid jobs, but ones that make you much happier than the higher paid and quite stressful job you may currently have. Here a real example of my ex-boss, now based in the UK. He asked me to be one of his challengers (you read right: my *boss* asked me to be one of *his* challengers... even that is possible[11]). He once spent some time in California, and he loved it very much. Further, his big dream was to be a scuba diver teacher at the Santa Monica Beach in California. Guess what: during my challenger session with him, when he told me that, I asked him: "So what are you doing here? If you love California and scuba diving so much, what in the world are you doing here in cloudy, windy, cold and rainy London...?" He answered: "I am married, have kids and a mortgage." That is of course a valid answer, but he also fell into the classic trap of not considering the decreasing cash burn-rate curve. Once I explained to him the above-mentioned concept of the cash burn-rate curve, he was speechless for at least one minute, starring at his life-cycle model to which we just added the burn-rate curve. I could see that his brain was running at 100% of CPU usage[12]. He realized that once his kids are adults and have their degrees, he will not require the same (high) salary anymore in his later life stage, the long-term life-cycle. This realization truly boosted his thinking process and opened up a funnel of ideas and so-called what-ifs[13]. We then jointly developed a plan which got him super-excited: once his kids are adults and have finished their University, he will go back to California and wants to work as a scuba diver teacher. What an objective!

Of course, you may argue that a decreasing cash burn-rate is not the case for everyone. That is right. Again, this is your PDP and therefore also your life-

---

[11] He liked the Swiss PDP Approach® and argued that it makes a lot of sense to have the inventor of the Swiss PDP Approach® as one oft the three challengers.

[12] This term comes from the IT industry. When opening a large application, the CPU (processor) of your computer temporarily reaches 100% of its maximum computing power – in other words, only this task is being treated, full focus, there is no time for something else. No distraction.

[13] What-Ifs are questions immediately triggered when one starts dreaming about something: What if I did idea x? What if I did project y?

cycle model. If you like the thought process of a cash burn-rate, then add it to your life-cycle model. If you do not like it or do not believe in it, then skip it. Up to you. You want to become the CEO of your own life, so make a call and decide. Whether or not you believe in the cash burn-rate curve thing, I argue that thinking a bit about how much money you may need in every stage of your life makes a lot of sense in any case.

5.2.2 What You Get from Your Life-Cycle Model

You will get excitement. And a motivation boost. Just look at my ex-boss in the UK. He did a reverse-engineering kind of thing, so he planted a future goal (going back to California and working as a scuba diver teacher) and then looked from his planted goal backwards to today asking himself the question: "What do I need to do (short-term and mid-term) in order to be able to make my dream come true?" Guess what: he started taking scuba diving courses. First the PADI [14] Open Water Diver, then the PADI Advanced Open Water Diver, followed by the PADI Rescue Diver, PADI Dive Master etc. You should have seen him coming to the office after this session every morning. I saw a different person. He had a meaningful and cool long-term goal in mind that kept him going and motivated for the at that time tough financial situation with family, kids and mortgage. But he had a plan and a motivating goal, and that changed him significantly. It was a truly transformative experience.

Your life-cycle model gives you a much better overview of what has to happen now, what can wait as well as any kind of dependencies between objectives. It helps you prioritize and make decisions. Please look at your own life-cycle model: does life not look much clearer now? Do you not feel that you now see

---

[14] *PADI is one of the world's leading scuba diver training organization.*
(https://www.padi.com)

the big picture (or see it better) and that you managed to connect the dots? Does it not feel great to have had external input and to have been challenged by others? Not everything has to be 100% clear now, as no one can plan every little detail in his or her life, but you should have made a significant step forward.

5.3 Step Three: Crafting Your Next Steps ⇒ Your Personal Development Plan

Congratulations on your life-cycle model version 3.0. You are almost there… the hard work is already done. What is missing? Crafting the next steps. That sounds easy, and it is, given your hard work on life-map and life-cycle-model, truly much easier now. Moreover, crafting next steps now is also more meaningful as you got to know yourself much better.

Step three is now really up to you. Based on the outcomes of step one and two, especially step two with its time dimension, you should have a clear idea what you want to start with next. Just bear in mind: it is not just about what you would like to do in the current life-cycle (aka the short-term life-cycle), that is pretty obvious. It is also about things that you would like to do later on, but which may require something else before. Example from my UK boss: if his dream is to become a scuba diver teacher in Santa Monica/California, that is not something that he can simply turn on later over night – that requires going through some preceding steps (e.g. Open Water Diver degree, Advanced Open Water Diver degree, Rescue Diver degree, Dive Master degree etc.). So a reasonable list of next steps usually includes a sound mix of truly short-term items as well as some prerequisites for mid-term and/or long-term objectives. Think about it. Connect the dots.

Also here, for the third and last time, I will show you a real example of a next step list, see below. This is the next step list of the same London-based Googler you have seen examples from beforehand. Again, this is just an example. Your list will look completely different.

Figure 22: Example of Real Next Steps

FYI it is not important that you can actually read what is written in Figure 22 – the notes are very individual and personal anyway. However, there is one take-away of Figure 22: do not focus on more than three things (besides your normal daily life like your job or your family duties) for a certain period of time. Focus is a prerequisite for GTD, so focus please. If you have too many things you would like to do, then just move some of them to the next life-cycle, or move it to next time you review your PDP, maybe in a year from now. No worries, your intentions and ideas will not be lost - just park some of them (in writing). Figure 22 shows that he focused on three areas (green titles) and then had either things that we wanted to do (e.g. keep travelling) or things that he wanted to clarify (the already known MBA vs. Master of Finance degree question).

Anyway, you will figure it out. Do not be afraid, just start crafting your next steps in a way that helps you. Make sure it is clear:

- <u>what</u> you want to do
- by <u>when</u> you want to do it
- <u>who</u> may help you with it
- and when you want to <u>review</u> your PDP (that is very very important... constancy and consistency are the key to success here, it is not a one-shot thing).

5.4   And Then?

Congratulations on your first Personal Development Plan following the Swiss PDP Approach®. You can be proud of yourself as most people do not actually steer their lives at all, many just go with the flow and do what is à la mode - whether they are aware of it or not. But not you! You just became the CEO of your life, you are now the captain of your life steering your life ship yourself, at least to certain degree. Of course, the unexpected always happens. However, you are much better prepared for whatsoever thanks to your PDP efforts. Now, you are by far more rooted because you got to know yourself better and you got challenged by other people in a systematic manner. You have built a solid foundation for your life, whatever comes. Congratulations again.

What you will do with the PDP outcome and how you will use it, is up to you – whether your share it with your boss[15] (or partner) or not, is your decision.

---

[15] depending on the level of trust

To make the best out of your PDP, I highly recommend the following:

- Review it regularly – at least once a year.
- Keep in contact with your challengers. You have established a precious relationship with them. More transformative experiences may happen thanks to additional talks with them in the future, so treat them well ☺.

5.5 PDP Pro: Some Advanced Tips

A lot of people do not suffer from not having numerous ideas, good intentions (whether they are well planned and well challenged or not) and/or lots of new-year resolutions. What is mostly missing is GTD (Getting-Things-Done). What counts is not just having good intentions, but actually doing something… getting a measurable output as well as real and sustainable results, right? This chapter intends to help you move from plans to results, from intentions to actions.

Do you like math? Functions? No worries, you will also get the point if you do not like mathematics at all. Nevertheless, let's start with a mini math excursion. You may remember your math teacher talking about functions, e.g.:

$$y(x) = 2x$$

In words: y is a function of x, where y = 2x. Example: if x = 3.5, then

$$y = 2x = 2 * 3.5 = \underline{7}$$

You may ask yourself: what in the world do functions have to do with a PDP? It is a fair question. The answer is: a lot. Not at first sight, but kind of between the lines. It is, by the way, another grandfather wisdom thing:

Expectations define to a very high degree the level of disappointment.

Back to math: The level of disappointment is therefore a function of expectations:

Disappointment (Expectations)

In words: the level or the degree of a person's disappointment is a function of the person's expectations. That means: it exists a high correlation between what the person's expectations were (beforehand) and the person's level of disappointment (afterwards). If you expect a lot, you may be disappointed more or more often. Simple, right? Of course, I do not want to influence you to reduce your audacious goals or to lower your expectations in general. It is good to have stretch goals to keep you awake and motivated, to bring you out of your comfort zone. For instance, I once read about a man suffering from asthma who was still capable of completing a marathon. Wow. Amazing. However, on the other hand, denying the reality and/or blaming others in case of failure (because you expected unrealistic things from people or from your environment in general) does not help, either. If you think going to a great school will get you the degree without a minimum level of hard work, then just forget about it. Got it? The intention of this paragraph is solely to make sure you have audacious but still realistic goals combined with decent and reasonable expectations.

Does it still sound quite academic and too theoretical? So here some real-life input. Sometimes, people blame everything and everyone for whatever – right?

If one does not pass a test, then it is either the school's fault, the teacher's fault, or even the fault of Minister of Education of the respective country – right? But it is, of course, never the person's own fault, not even partially. Or if someone is stuck in traffic jam, then it is the crystal clear fault of all the other drivers, because they all could have left their houses earlier or later. They think the entire world is wrong (like a ghost driver), and they are the only ones being right and being smart. What a misconception. You get the point. You may also think that is a bit exaggerated - you are right, but just a bit. First, exaggeration often helps make a point, it is an intellectual game in order to better see where a trend is heading to. Second, these people truly exist. Without noticing, they are in a very dangerous situation as they suffer from ostrichism[16], aka denial of reality. Do not blame the entire world for not having achieved something. It may make you feel good for a moment, but you do not fix the root cause of the problem at all. Again, there are of course some things that are beyond a person's control, and they have to be taken into account and managed. In their HBR article, Michael Watkins and Max Bazerman (2003) beautifully distinguish between *true surprises* and *predictable surprises*[17]. If you feel that most road-blockers in your life are beyond your control, then I highly recommend reading their article or even their book (*Predictable Surprises: The Disasters You Should Have Seen Coming, and How to Prevent Them*[18]).

---

[16] *The term ostrichism comes from the animal ostrich who is famous for burying the head in the sand if case of danger (whether this is actually true or a myth is apparently not 100% clear).*

[17] *https://hbr.org/2003/04/predictable-surprises-the-disasters-you-should-have-seen-coming*

[18] *ISBN-13: 9781591391784*

5.5.1 Advanced Tip #1: Do Not Fall in the Ostrichism Trap

How to figure out if you also suffer (a bit) from ostrichism? Very easy, just do the following exercise for a while, and you will figure it out: during a couple of days, write down precisely every little thing you complain about. Then, after a couple of days, look at the list and do a reality check yourself... does it sound like the examples mentioned above? While this exercise does not solve any problem itself, it does for sure one thing for you: it opens your eyes and you will not waste time blaming others anymore, but start spending time on the concrete problem solving. It will align yourself with the real world, and that is already a good thing ☺.

5.5.2 Advanced Tip #2: Getting Things Done Thanks to Post-Its

It is very easy to have a nice PDP hidden somewhere – be in on a hard drive, in the cloud or on hardcopy in a drawer. In other words: after having completed your PDP, you may easily hide yourself from your own projects and objectives, you may get distracted or may even end up in the hamster wheel of your daily stuff. So how to make sure you turn your objectives into actions (GTD)? One simple recommendation is using the well-known and old-school post-its. Even in a digitized world, they have a place in our society – right here, for instance. Let's imagine you would like to lose weight – there is no better thing (in addition to advanced tip #3...) than putting a post-it with your weight loss objective right on the door of your fridge – just next to the door handle... sneaky, right? To make a long story short: make your objectives visible. Post-Its are a good way of doing it, but it is of course up to you, Mr/Ms/Mrs CEO of your own life, how you would like to make your objectives visible. You choose how to, but just <u>do</u> it. Visualize your objectives as much as possible.

5.5.3 Advanced Tip #3: Getting Things Done Thanks to Friends & Peer Pressure

Another truly powerful tip is telling as many people as possible about the things you want to achieve by when. It may make you feel a bit uncomfortable temporarily, but... Do you remember Chapter 2.1 about Hurt and Rescue? You will increase the pressure on yourself as your friends or peers know about your goals. That is a good thing, as there is virtually no way of escaping anymore. Even better: a lot of people will encourage you or support you in case of a temporary crisis (in which you alone might give up your undertaking...). You do not have to do everything yourself. Be smart. Smart people use the help of other people where reasonable and necessary. Of course, you should not massively over-announce things and then only deliver 5% of them. However, announce your game-changer goals, the ones which will move the needle.

5.5.4 Advanced Tip #4: Suggested Reading to Boost Your PDP

First things first: No, I do not get any commission for recommending the following two books. They just helped me a great deal in my professional life and supported the design and fine-tuning of the Swiss PDP Approach® as well.

The first one I have already mentioned earlier: Cal Newport's *Deep Work* (2016). His book is a true eye-opener for any knowledge worker and shows step-by-step what knowledge workers should do (and how...) in order to have jobs in the future. He wisely distinguishes between shallow work (= easily replicable work, soon be done by robots or algorithms) and deep work (= tasks where the human brain can shine and still nowadays outperforms the best supercomputer by far). Once you have read his book, you will not only understand what deep work is, but also why it is crucial and finally how to do it.

The second book is Carol S. Dweck's *Mindset* (2012), in my opinion also a must-read for knowledge workers in today's world of constant change. Lifelong learning is a well-known term, no doubt about it, but *how to do it* is not so obvious. Even some teachers have not fully understood how to enable kids and students for lifelong learning. Instead, they still make them study to know items by heart (= load things into the short-term memory) for the next exam and then make them forget it rapidly (= unload the memory) in order load new things into their short-term memory. By the way, that is one type of shallow work, where nothing really meaningful can arise, and dots are not connected at all. A waste of time. People do that just to pass an exam, but not really to understand something. They neither learn something new nor do they get the big picture. According to Dweck, these people have a fixed mindset. In her book, she distinguishes between a fixed mindset and a growth mindset and explains in an impressive way full of examples why a growth mindset is exponentially better. Further, she illustrates what it takes to get a growth mindset and that intelligence is not given by birth. You will see: having a growth mindset is a game changer[19]!

Once you have read both books (or at least their summaries), you will realize that deep work requires a growth mindset and vice versa. Equipped with the wisdom and practical recommendations from Newport and Dweck, you will definitely boost your PDP to *PDP pro* status.

5.6 Would You Like to Get a Video Training for Your PDP Process?

No problem at all. It is free of charge. Just go to www.swiss-pdp-approach.com and watch the training video.

---

[19] *Dweck's Stanford article diagram explains the difference between a fixed mindset and a growth mindset in a minute:*

http://alumni.stanford.edu/content/magazine/artfiles/dweck_2007_2.pdf

That's it. There is nothing more I have to say. We are done. Now it is up to you. Make your intentions happen. Review them. Make other things happen. Keep going. Learn. Grow. Steer your life. Enjoy!

6 One-Pager: Swiss PDP Approach® Process Overview

Figure 23 summarizes the entire Swiss PDP Approach® on one page. You may print it out (go to www.swiss-pdp-approach.com) and have it next to you when reading the book, and/or have it next to you during your PDP process. That way, you always know:

- where you are
- what is next
- who should support you
- what the outcome is supposed to be

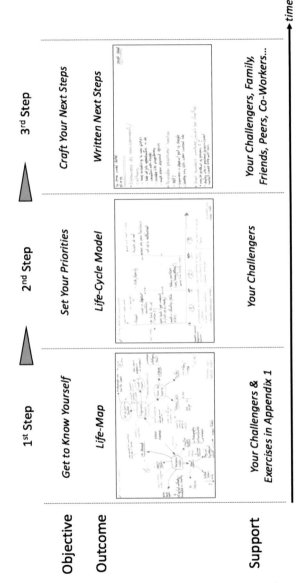

Figure 23: Process Overview of Swiss PDP Approach®

7 Q&A

Here is a collection of the most common and typical PDP questions I have gathered over the last ten years working and refining the Swiss PDP Approach® around the world. If you cannot find the answer to your question, please let me now: beat.buhlmann@gmail.com.

Q: The **development approach at my company** seems to be much more serious, apparently having more meat on the bone as I have to fill out a form with about 250 questions. Further, I get a nicely-looking three-dimensional diagram or a multi-branch spider diagram, about 40 pages in total. Is the Swiss PDP Approach® not too simple to be effective?

A: *I recommend that you use the material you got from your company's approach during Swiss PDP Approach®. Please do not throw it away. I am sure it contains a lot of valuable information. In a nutshell, my tip is to <u>combine</u> both.*

We all know: Simplicity is key. My PDP approach looks very simple at first sight (just three steps), but the process of going through the three steps is quite rich. My experience with companies offering a process like the one you just described is that most people get lost and finally do not do anything at all. Give the Swiss PDP Approach® a try.

Q: How can I **find** good **challengers**?

A: *First of all: Take some time, you are not in a rush. Good challengers are key to your PDP's success.*

Make sure you find challengers with different backgrounds. People who know you from different points of view, or from different phases of your life. Find people who are well known for telling the truth, even if it may not always be nice or flattering what they have to say. These people are worth a mint. Another recommendation: get a good mix of people, not only regarding life experience, but also with regards to education and degrees. Sometimes, people with no degrees have an amazing level of wisdom (e.g. my grandfather). Be smart and choose wisely. Answering your question: just ask them. Tell them that they have been chosen by you for reason x or y. It may even flatter them a bit (would it not flatter you a bit when being asked?)

Q: **Will the challengers** not **laugh** at me when I ask them?

A: *Believe it or not: I have not heard one single case over the last ten years where people told me that potential challengers said no or even laughed. The opposite was the case: besides being flattered a bit for being asked/chosen, they are usually very impressed by the PDP idea in general. Many of them even start their own PDP process afterwards. I have heard statements like "Hmmm. I should have done this kind of thing 20 years ago...". So, no worries. Just ask them. Make sure it is a good moment to talk about it, e.g. while having a coffee, maybe lunch or dinner. Also, either print some of the PDP information so you can show something, or bring the book to the meeting. That helps them understand what it is that you ask them to do.*

Q: What do I **tell** my potential **challengers**?

A: *See Q&A above, plus: tell them that <u>you</u> want to get to know yourself better, and that you need <u>their</u> help to do so – e.g. to detect blind spots.*

Most people react in a very impressed (positive) manner. Also, tell them that you would like to learn from their life experience.

Q: **I have a partner** (wife, husband, boyfriend, girlfriend etc.): What do I tell my partner? Anything at all?

A: *Absolutely. Well, it actually depends on the quality of the relationship, to be honest... but thinking positively: yes, tell it. Absolutely. Tell them what you plan to do and why. Best would be if both partners went through such a process. It will result in a much more solid foundation for your relationship. Further, it is up to you if you choose your partner as one of the challengers or not (I suggest it, but it is up to you).*

One PDP training participant told me after he had completed his life-map: "Beat, I cannot show this to my wife, she would freak out seeing what is written on my life-map." Well, that is, in my humble opinion, already a strong sign that the relationship is far from ideal... I strongly believe that such a relationship will break up sooner or later anyway. => The fact of having done a PDP and sharing it with your partner does not <u>break</u> a relationship, it simply brings already <u>existing issues to the surface</u>.

What did I tell him? I said: "It is like a wildfire... it is much easier and less costly to extinguish a small fire then a huge wildfire." He got the point.

Q: If I **do not want not share** my life-map or life-cycle model **with my manager** – does it still make sense to talk to him about professional development?

A: *Absolutely. You do <u>not need</u> to share your life-map or your life-cycle-model with your manager, unless you feel comfortable to do so. It requires a certain level of mutual trust. It is a good sign if it is possible, of course. However, what everyone can do is using the output of your PDP process when talking to the manager. During the PDP process, you have learned a lot about yourself, your no-gos, your aspirations and wishes etc. You also have a better idea about timing and milestones. So, only share as much information of what you have discovered during your PDP journey as you want. Your manager may not 100% understand why you want to do (or do not want to do) a certain thing, but he will surely realize and feel that your thoughts are well rooted.*

Q: As a **manager**, I am a bit worried to propose and support PDPs because once a team member has completed the process, there might be a high risk of losing him/her. Reason: My team member might figure out that the current job does not fit him/her at all and quit – so is it actually not **better to try to prevent people from doing PDPs**?

A: *Good question. Think twice about what you just said. Are you (just) a manager or a leader?*

Yes, it is possible that people might change the job or even leave the company – so what? Do you want to work with not highly motivated people? You will reach your mid-term and long-term goals much better if you have the <u>right person</u> in the <u>right role</u>. Yes, it may mean that you have to hire a new person, so you probably have to go through an entire hiring process. Welcome to real life.

From a big picture point of view: Success in a company is like playing soccer: "it is a team thing"[20]. You as the coach of a soccer team cannot win, you need a highly motivated bunch of people, and each of them needs to be in the right position. Do not put a striker in the position of a goalie and vice versa.

Some people may not like the next part of the answer, but I will say it anyway (=> hurt and rescue). I argue that if you still believe that it is good to try to prevent people from doing a PDP, or to prevent them from generally thinking about their lives and if they are in the right role, then you are neither a leader (maybe a short-term and bonus-focused manager) nor a good people manager. People managers care about people, that is why they are called people manager. Think about it. Did you become a people manager just to get to the next salary level? Do you actually enjoy working with people? Now, we are in the middle of a life-map challenger discussion ☺.

Last but not least: this kind of thinking might also indicate a fixed mindset. I therefore recommend you read 5.5.4 'Advanced Tip #4: Suggested Reading to Boost Your PDP' again.

Q: I am still a bit **confused**, I think I did not really get it yet. I am more of a visual person when learning something new by reading, I prefer video trainings. Can you help me?

A: *No worries, there is a video explaining the entire process step-by-step. Just go to www.swiss-pdp-approach.com watch the video training. Enjoy!*

---

[20] *Quoting the CEO of Evernote, Chris O'Neill, September 2016*

Q: We all know that **nobody** can **entirely plan** the own **life**. So many things happen unforeseen. So is a PDP not just a huge waste of time?

A: *Important question. Short answer: It is not a waste of time, not at all! Longer answer: Imagine pilot training. Pilots get trained for hundreds of hours to be able to deal with as many tough situations as possible – even though every real situation in itself is unique. Would you still say that pilots should not be trained in simulators because the training does not cover 100% of everything they will have to go through? Surely not. Having a decent PDP does not mean that you entirely plan your life in all details. However, it means that you first get to know yourself better (the foundation), then think thoroughly about your dreams and wishes, no-gos, issues & challenges, and finally get challenged by others. It is a framework helping you approach life management at least to a certain degree, but it also leaves you with enough flexibility to react to whatever may happen or occur during your life. I argue that having a solid PDP prepares much better for whatever may come, especially for the unplanned events (also the mid-life crisis), thanks to the solid foundation you built and the big picture view you gained during the entire PDP journey. Last but not least, I recommend you read 5.5.4 'Advanced Tip #4: Suggested Reading to Boost Your PDP' again.*

Q: I am a **people manager** and quite **nervous** about the **reaction of my team member** during the upcoming PDP meeting. I know that he wants to move on with his career and become a people manager, but I cannot offer such a role to him right now or soon. As we work in a small company, there are not so many opportunities as one may have in a large corporation. He is a good team member and for sure capable of becoming a people manager, no doubt. I do not want to lose him. How should I react?

A: *You mention a very important point: As a people manager, you can neither change the reality nor can you change facts. However, what you <u>can</u> do is helping him deal with the situation. In your particular case, for instance, you may tell him that a manager role promotion is currently not possible and you explain why. It is not because you do not want this to happen, but because there is simply no such role available at the moment. Give him the real picture, even if it hurts. Important: Do not stop here. Help him by showing him options what he could do in the meantime to fine-tune his skill set. He might work on a particular weakness that he should better fix or improve before he gets promoted to a people manager, or he might learn another language to get an even more interesting people manager role within your company later on, e.g. in another country. You may also give him some special projects which will train him for his first people manager role. In any case, as long as you keep helping him, even if it is just with ideas what could be done, he will realize that you care. Moreover, it may also be helpful to share your own example of becoming a people manager, maybe you also had to wait a bit. Show appreciation.*

8 References

Dweck, Carol S. 2012, *Mindset - Updated Edition: Changing The Way You Think to Fulfil Your Potential,* Hachette UK, ISBN 1780-33393-5 & 9781780333939

Mull, John Stuart 1859, *On Liberty,* Harvard University, W. Parker and Son, digitized Nov 9th 2007

Newport, Cal 2016, *Deep Work: Rules for Focused Success in a Distracted World,* Grand Central Publishing, ISBN 1455-58666-8 & 978-1455-58666-0

Watkins, Michael & Bazerman, Max 2003, *Predictable Surprises: The Disasters You Should Have Seen Coming,* Harvard Business Review 81 (3): 72-80, 140

9   Appendix One: Exercises to Find Out Who You Are

The following exercises are from Tania Konnerth, a German psychologist. It is her intellectual property, not mine. Below her exercises translated from German to English.

Who am I? Finding Out Who You Are.   *By Tania Konnerth*[21]

Self-knowledge and getting to know yourself is a long and intensive personal journey. I can only provide you with some ideas encouraging you to find out more about yourself and to look at yourself in a positive way. It makes it much easier to accept yourself as who you are and avoids pretending to be someone you may aspire to be but who you are simply not. *The following three exercises may support your life-map version 1.0 before you meet your challengers*[22].

---

1) Basic Exercise to Start With

A basic exercise for self-knowledge is writing your resume. Take the appropriate amount of time to write your resume as a continuous text, in bullet points, on index cards or whatever you feel is appropriate. You do not have to put things in chronological order, just let it be freely flowing. You may find out new and astonishing insights by reading your own CV again.

---

[21] *source: http://www.zeitzuleben.de/wer-bin-ich-herausfinden-wer-man-ist/*

[22] *This sentence in italics was added by the author, Beat Buhlmann*

2) Going Deeper

Below you will find a series of questions that will help you learn more about yourself:

- How would you describe yourself to someone who does not know you?
- What are your strengths?
- What have been your biggest successes?
- What are you really proud of in your life and why? And what not?
- What are the different roles you currently hold in life?
- What do you enjoy versus what do you find draining?
- The three things that you like to do most are ...
- What are your three wishes?
- What do you want others to say about you and the life you lived?

Recognizing Your Beliefs

Complete the following sentences as spontaneously as possible:

Life is... Having to die means... Human beings can ... Human beings should... The world needs.... The most important thing(s) in life is/are... The past was... The presence means... The future is... Love means... To have friends is.... "Luck" means to me... Hope means... I believe in... I have the courage to.... I have faith in... I fear ...Work means to me .... Money is.... My strengths are ... My weaknesses...

Questions About Your Childhood

Complete the following sentence and answer the questions:

- I was the only one in the family to always ...
- If your parents had had a banner in your home when you were a child, what would it have said?
- What was clearly forbidden by your parents when you were a child?
- What was the thing that your parents mostly encouraged you to do when you were a child?
- What is your earliest memory from childhood?
- How would you describe your childhood (buzzwords, short)?
- What was sad or bad for you as a child and why?
- What was your favorite story as a child and why?
- What was your favorite game and why?
- Did you have an imaginary friend as a child?
- What was your happiest time as a child and why?

---

3) Looking Backward from the Future: Your 80th Birthday Exercise

The exercise 'your 80th birthday' helps you look at your personal value system in a clearer way.

Imagine a grand celebration of your 80th birthday

Imagine it is your 80th birthday and there is a big celebration in your honor. You sit in a comfortable chair and enjoy the fact that many people have come to your big celebration. All guests will talk with you and congratulate you personally as you are the center of the evening. Imagine this situation calmly. Visualize it. You may want to close your eyes.

Four people make a speech about you
After the banquet, all your guests are happy and satisfied. Some want to give your visitors a little speech. The following four people are going to talk about you - about your life, about the significance you have in their life and the positive impact you have made.

- someone from your family,
- a good friend,
- a co-worker and
- someone from the city or municipality where you live, for example, the mayor.

Think: What do you want these people to say about you?
These four people will talk about you. What would you like to hear? It is not about what they would say about you currently, but your vision about what you would like them to say. The ultimate question is: What do you want other people to say about you and about your life? What will others think of you when you are 80 years old? This may have a strong influence on what you are going to do in the future and what not.

With this exercise, you often find your personal values
Do you know what you would want people to say about your accomplishments and personality when giving a toast on your 80th birthday? Many people are not aware of the fact that a lot is about their values (honesty, loyalty, etc.) and not necessarily about a clear objective.

If you know your values, it easier to find your goals

Once you are clear about your values, you are able to define your goals. If you want to be 'helpful', you can engage in some neighborhood initiative or similar. If you want to be famous, you would have to think about what you would want to be famous for. For example, if you aim to be a famous actor, your objective would be to become an actor – of course.

Important: your goals must not contradict your values

It is also very important to know which personal values you have. Only if you know your personal values, you can prevent yourself from selecting goals that are contrary to your values. Otherwise, it may happen that you set goals that are counterproductive to what is really important to you - that would be a true self-sabotage. Comparing your goals with your values should become a regular exercise.

Example of 'Your 80th Birthday' Exercise

Mr. X wrote down the following (in parenthesis are the personal values he listed)

My son says about me:
- I was there for him (willingness to help and act as a good father),
- I took him seriously (respect),
- I was sympathetic and tolerant (tolerance),
- I have tried to understand him, even if it was hard for me (understanding, tolerance).

My good friend Karl says about me:
- We shared a lot of good times (fun)
- I could be taken seriously (serious)

- He appreciates my sense of humor and wit (humor)
- I was there for him when he needed me (to help, a good friend), and;
- I was a loyal and reliable friend, even though we sometimes had disagreements (reliability, friendship).

My former colleague Ricardo says about me:
- I have always tried to improve things at work (productivity & responsibility),
- I helped him solve problems and helped understand the root cause (problem solving),
- I have always been able to arbitrate in a dispute (peace, harmony), and
- I am thoroughly reliable, but was never a stickler for principles (reliability, accuracy, flexibility).

The mayor of my city says about me:
- I was a helpful and responsible citizen (responsibility),
- I have been involved with the community (helpfulness), and
- My generous donations helped make the city a more beautiful and better place (generosity).

Example of concrete goals of this exercise

Mr. X set out his goal to be a good father. He then set the goal to seek, together with his son, a hobby they would both enjoy and spend time together. He has further recognized that it is important to be socially engaged and helpful so he set a target starting next month to volunteer two hours a week with the elderly.

<u>Example of how personal values and goals may contradict each other</u>

Mrs. Y found that family 'is a very important value for her'. As Mrs. Y wrote down her goals, she set a target to become head of her department. She checked her goal to see if it came into conflict with her values and quickly discovered that her family value is not really compatible with her career goals. She now knows that she has to find a way to combine her goal with the importance she places on family. Having this clarity will help her make better decisions.

Complete this exercise to better understand your values <u>and</u> how closely - or not - you actually live them.
